MOSS-HUNG TREES

HAIKU

of the west coast

by award winner
Winona Baker

calligraphy by Christine McKim

Moss-Hung Trees
HAIKU of the West Coast

Copyright © 1992 by Winona Baker

Cover illustration: Delia Becker

Published by
REFLECTIONS
P.O. Box 178
Gabriola, B.C. V0R 1X0
Canada

Canadian Cataloguing in Publication Data

Baker, Win, 1924-
Moss-hung trees

ISBN 0-9692570-3-1

    1. Haiku, Canadian (English) 2. Canadian poetry (English)—20th century 3. British Columbia —Poetry. I. Title.

PS8553.A3855M6 1992
PR9199.3.B34M6 1992
C811'.54
C92-091047-5

To Don and Mary

ACKNOWLEDGEMENTS

Haiku of Winona Baker have appeared in the following publications:

Alchemist
Alberta Poetry Yearbooks 1984, '87, '88
Discovery
Frogpond
Hai
Haiku Canada Sheets
Haiku Zasshi Zo
HI: Haiku International
International Naiku Work Collection 1987
Mainichi Daily News, Japan
Mirrors
Modern Haiku
New Cicada
Poetry Review
1991 Ituen Tea Haiku Contest
World Haiku Contest Work Collection 1989
Writer's Quarterly

Anthologies:

A Fall of Leaves
Haiku Canada Anthologies
Milkweed

Books by the author:

Clouds Empty Themselves, 1987 Red Cedar Press, Nanaimo B.C.
Not so Scarlet a Woman, 1987 Red Cedar Press, Nanaimo B.C.

A Faint Gash on Time

"Haiku is simply what is happening in this place, at this moment."
— Matsuo Basho

"A haiku...puts forth images reflecting intuitions."
— Daisetz Szuki

HAIKU is an intuitive response to a direct experience with nature. Transcendent time, when nature and human nature become one, is sketched in the present tense even if the action happened in the past. Seemingly unrelated things may be juxtaposed, but no explanations, moralizing or judgements are made. Haiku holds the mirror to nature and the experience is revealed.

Today, old styles are not always followed and many haiku change at least one. Traditional texts describe haiku as Japanese seasonal verse having 17 syllables arranged in three lines of 5, 7, 5 syllables. Counting syllables is an example of guidelines often ignored because Japanese syllables are not the same as ours (something many early translators did not understand). What can be said in one breath is a better guide than counting. One line, one word haiku have been written. "Invisible poem" defines the haiku moment.

Haiku is objective and avoids many Western poetic devices. R.H. Blyth said that a "jewelled" finger or a "deformed" finger distracts from what it points at. Haiku is a poetry of nouns. Invest in them, as b.p. nichol advised, with the power they have. Modifiers, similes, metaphors, and end rhyme do not belong in haiku.

Season can be stated or implied by the use of "kigo", a season word. Daffodil could be kigo for spring in some places and haiku poets (haijin) have many of these words. Some western writers have begun compiling kigo applicable to today's times and different geographical areas. Winter words for the coast of British Columbia are not winter words in the Yukon or California.

Haiku is meant to be enjoyed and appreciated. It has been written during festivals, parties, nature tours, walks and other delightful diversions. Historically, the idea of foreigners writing haiku did not please all Japanese. They felt the languages, sensibilities, and philosophies of western countries were so different from theirs that "aborted flowers" would best describe any such attempts!

Today, however, Japanese corporations, foundations, and haiku associations encourage the writing of haiku worldwide, a voice to the spirit of union when nature and human nature become one. That moment, which sharpens our awareness of the natural world around us and our inseparable relationship to it, is without boundaries.

Haiku is, as Roland Barthe writes, "a faint gash on time."

>In the midst of the plain
>Sings the skylark
>Free of all things
>— Matsuo Basho

Winona Baker
February, 1991

Table of Contents

1 Spring

   Summer   *15*

33 Autumn

   Winter   *47*

Spring

two bald eagles
in two trees
watch our boat

first warm day
mother lets down hems
of summer dresses

piano keys move fingers
nesting bird outside
never a wrong note

spring girls walk in malls
old men on benches watching
fall in love again

strutting young men
glare at old men
girl watching

tree screened river
two blue heron battle
the rain is green

startled red tulips
bloom in concrete boxes
signalling help

purple violets
beneath the monkey tree
again

he plays a flute
in moonlit fields
to help seeds grow

mouse
in the garter snake's jaws
screaming spring

apple tree
if no one watched
would petals fall?

laburnum drip yellow
dogwood whisper white
aching spring

the way
the foal tries clover
returns to milk

round white nubbins
coming through the loam
Indian pipes - ghost flowers

yellow monarch
helicopters over lawn
the grapes are green

squirrel
still pursues her
tail half gone

crowded bus
sweating placental mammals
and a butterfly

gardener
hangs bags of human hair
to keep deer away

through the trees
hiding the ocean
sea lions bark

forest hike in spring
on the ground fresh cougar scat
bristling with deer hair

Summer

dedication
a new picnic shelter
it starts to rain

"Don't pick wild flowers!"
Marj focuses her camera
to gift me again

blue puddle
gull appears
disappears

postcard blue ocean
Gabriola's grey cliffs
orca leaps

leave the ferry
they won't explore the island
want to build a raft

downtown cathedral
white roses cartwheel
to the sidewalk

woman in the park
you make your child a jewel
wearing him in front

city sunlight
the blind girl
staring at noise

what would happen if
all that concrete tumbled
blackberries would grow

summer zoo: Dianne
ignores bars and cages
for daisies in grass

above Cameron Lake
a vagrant white mist
explores the mountain

summer trail
a trashed car in the salal
rusting in peace

finally the lake
bend to drink
drowned cougar kit

huge toad
in small cupped hands
"Aren't his bumps cute?"

deserted rest stop
wild flowers grace the table
thank-you unknown host

picnic at the river
where wolves came down the mountain
became human

summer hawk
above small boat
endless sky

hotsprings
sit in them and look
toward Japan

August heat
the roadside daisies
smell of dust

pub's neon lights
luring boats
in the harbour

father drinks his beer
mother and daughter battle
smoke - wreathed heads

Miss Nude Canada
gyrates on the damp stage
rhinestone noise

pitcher of beer
tossed garter falls in
splash!

my son
and his son
wade into their shadows

all the flowers cropped
they came so silently
the black-tailed deer

left at the base
of the world's tallest totem
a throwaway diaper

sunlit Adam
lying on the small bridge
tries to pat koi fish

headlights
reflected in the deer's eyes
the leap

Autumn

moss - hung trees
a deer moves into
the hunter's silence

Winner of the Japanese Foreign Minister's Grand Prize
(international section) in the World Haiku Contest
Yamagata, Japan   July 15, 1989

hunter stood
at the sea and sang
calling the whale

                        sun in the east
                        geese fly into
                        the western moon

my daughter cartwheels
between me and
the setting sun

white dogwood
a second blossoming
as leaves turn red

old graveyard
a student doing rubbings
wild geese cry

Gallows Point
the lighthouse blinks
where men were hung

ripening corn
whispers taffeta secrets
a warm moon

Indian summer
green dies in the leaves
sun sets

two empty rockers
silver-plated
by the moon

graveyard poplar
bumps and grinds in the wind
shedding yellow leaves

one month in school
she smells of chalk dust
and erudition

one two three four five
sailboats in the fog
between land and island

autumn cleanup
in house and garden
sun's last rays

moonlit children
scatter among the headstones
playing frozen tag

dry October
this river should be full
of spawning salmon

folded wings
loon enters lake
no splash no sound

too late
November rains
the fish whose spawn are gone

Winter

twisted arbutus
carving waves
attack the rock

she tells stories
there were drumming gooey ducks
and dancing salmon

                    killer whale swam
                    up the inlet to carry
                    the dead soul away

chair lift rises
we reach the mountain top
strange look down on trees

the tractor rolls
over sheets of plywood
on the graveyard grass

black birds wheel
in front of grey clouds
moving in the wind

    the moon is cold
     around the porch light
    no moth flutters

the crippled crow
hops on the icy edge
of the compost box

rain torn letters
in the mailman's hands
black raincape smiles

heavy winter rain
green things beaten down
and things not green

winter maple
stripped of everything
but a blue kite

mind grandchildren
my son's divorce final
winter day

sunrise
a child's plastic wheelbarrow
red in the snow

who can
withstand the rain
only these green conifers

teaching haiku
a class of boys
it starts to snow

snow burdened town
robin eats holly berries
no one calls

toppled fir
it made the kitchen dark
but.....

he brings in cold
a perfect snowflake melts
in his dark hair

baby in heaven
rides his father's back
skaters on the lake

a white kitten plays
in her long dark hair
she scolds in Wakashan

specter trees
where a beaver dam
flooded this forest

snowflakes fill
the eye of the eagle
fallen totem pole